Original title:
The Art of Reverie

Copyright © 2024 Swan Charm Publishing
All rights reserved.

Editor: Jessica Elisabeth Luik
Author: Luise Luik
ISBN HARDBACK: 978-9916-86-138-7
ISBN PAPERBACK: 978-9916-86-139-4

In the Silence of the Mind

Amidst the chaos, soft whispers call,
In silent corners, echoes fall.
A thought unspoken, gently twined,
Dwells deep in the silence of the mind.

Silent rivers of dreams flow free,
In the quiet, deep reverie.
Untold stories by time consigned,
Weave, unseen, in the silence of the mind.

Beneath the stars, where shadows play,
Silent musings find their way.
Wisps of memories, intertwined,
Are dancing in the silence of the mind.

Silent Crescendo

In the stillness, music grows,
Unheard symphonies in repose.
A crescendo, silent, finely lined,
Blooms within the heart's confine.

Morning dew, a quiet plea,
Whispers secrets to the tree.
Silent cadence, undefined,
Awakes within the heart and mind.

On the breeze, a hush, divine,
Carries tunes of the sublime.
In each heartbeat, you'll find,
A silent crescendo intertwined.

In Heartfelt Echoes

Gentle murmurs, soft embrace,
Echoes travel, heart's sweet place.
In a whisper, so aligned,
Linger in heartfelt echoes designed.

Love's reflection, doubling too,
Reaches far and follows through.
In love's whispers, so refined,
Resides in heartfelt echoes confined.

Timeless words, through ages aired,
In the heart, forever shared.
Silent echoes, hearts combined,
Live forever in echoes of the kind.

Moments Beneath the Surface

Hidden moments, slight and fair,
Dreams unravel, unaware.
Beneath the surface, thoughts combined,
Dive deep, where secrets are enshrined.

Every ripple, softly fading,
Layers cloaked, always shading.
In still waters, minds aligned,
With moments beneath the surface, intertwined.

Silent depths, where feelings hide,
Unseen currents, far and wide.
In the quiet, undefined,
Lie moments beneath the surface, combined.

Journey Through Tranquil Scenes

Whispers of the gentle breeze,
Rustling through ancient trees.
Footfalls light on sodden ground,
In this peace, my soul is found.

Rivers weave a silver thread,
Through the valleys quiet spread.
Mountains stand as silent guards,
Nature's beauty, heaven's cards.

Petals soft beneath the feet,
Where the earth and sky do meet.
Birdsong echoes through the air,
Binding time in moments rare.

In these tranquil scenes I rove,
Seeking treasures to uncover.
In the spaces wide and free,
Here my heart forever be.

Spirit Walk Through Timeless Fields

Dew upon the morning grass,
Soothing as the hours pass.
Every step a gentle way,
Toward the dawning of the day.

Fields that stretch in endless hues,
Kissed by soft and golden views.
Memories in breezes flow,
In these fields, my spirits grow.

Shadows from the ancient trees,
Dance in rhythm with the breeze.
Whispered tales from ages gone,
In their roots, the stories drawn.

Moon above the quiet ground,
As the day fades with no sound.
In this timeless, whispered lore,
I find myself once more.

Lost Amongst the Reveries

Dreams arise on silken thread,
Stories spun and gently spread.
Wandering through the twilight's glow,
In this realm we softly flow.

Stars align in mystic dance,
Guiding through the vast expanse.
Every step a door to past,
Moments fleeting, never last.

Wandering where dreams reside,
In the corners where they hide.
Each a glimpse of silent tales,
In this space where spirit sails.

Lost amongst the reveries,
Where the heart its own will sees.
In this realm of endless night,
Finds the dawn in purest light.

Tender Glows of Moonlit Paths

Softly falls the evening's veil,
Silvered light on whispered trail.
Moon above in quiet grace,
Illuminates the gentle space.

Steps that echo on the stone,
Feel the night's embrace alone.
Shadows dance with tender sway,
Guiding through the twilight's play.

Paths that wind through ancient grove,
Every turn a tale of love.
In the stillness, dreams unfold,
Stories of the heart retold.

Moonlight's touch on every leaf,
Soothes the soul, dispels the grief.
Walking through this silent night,
Hearts are healed in tender light.

Fragments of the Midday Moon

In the sky the moon stands still,
Sunlit fragments, scattered light.
Echoes from a distant hill,
Blend their whispers with our sight.

Day and night in one embrace,
Shadows dance on beams of gold.
Silent stories interlace,
Midday secrets now unfold.

Time a tapestry unwound,
Every thread a sigh of noon.
In this symphony profound,
Fragments of the midday moon.

Lost in Whispered Breezes

Through the meadow, soft they glide,
Breezes whisper tales of old.
Every leaf a clue to hide,
Secrets that the winds have told.

Gentle fingers wake the grass,
Kiss the petals of the bloom.
Time in endless whispers pass,
Wrapped in nature's quiet loom.

Paths unseen lead hearts astray,
In the wind they find their tune.
Lost in breezes, fade away,
Dreams beneath the whispered moon.

Solitary Flights

Above the world they soar alone,
Wings unfurl in silent grace.
Carving dreams in skies unknown,
In the vast, uncharted space.

Whispers of the morning dew,
Echo in the flight of one.
Shadows lost in skies of blue,
Chasing dawn till day is done.

Lonely flight, yet not unseen,
Every path a quest for more.
In the solitary sheen,
Freedom found, forever soar.

Vignettes of Inner Peace

Quiet moments paint the day,
Brushstrokes soft, a heart's release.
In the silence, whispers play,
Crafting vignettes of inner peace.

Candles flicker, shadows blend,
Harmony in stillness found.
Spirit mends, begins to mend,
In the calm, no greater sound.

Breath by breath, a gentle weave,
Tapestry of tranquil trees.
In this space, we find reprieve,
Vignettes sailed on whispered seas.

Quixotic Corners

In quixotic corners where shadows play,
Winds whisper secrets of distant day,
The dreams of giants in a twilight hue,
Meld with the echoes of skies once blue.

The moonlight dances on cobblestone streets,
While stars above pulse to ancient beats,
A knight's lost gaze adrift through time,
In search of rhymes and reason's climb.

By candle's flicker in the midnight town,
Hope weaves its yarn in golden brown,
The world, it breathes a sigh of grace,
A fleeting glance of a tender face.

With every step through night's embrace,
Lies a promise in the hidden space,
Of battles fought and love unspoken,
Within the heart that remains unbroken.

Celestial Daydreams

Beneath the canvas of a starry sky,
Wonders drift as daytime bids goodbye,
Constellations weave their ageless lore,
Guiding us to realms we can explore.

The galaxy hums a lullaby's tune,
Guardians of night, the silent moon,
Through ether's veil, dreams take flight,
Spanning worlds in the velvet night.

Eyes closed tight in a cosmic trance,
Through milky waves, spirits dance,
A symphony of light, a gentle stream,
Flowing through the heart's daydream.

Beyond the horizon where suns sleep,
Secret realms in shadows creep,
Whispers of ancients, softly conveyed,
In celestial dreams night serenades.

Opalescent Contemplations

In an opalescent dawn's first light,
Shimmer thoughts take gentle flight,
Reflections dance on morning's face,
A tranquil start in time's embrace.

Pearlescent hues of wisps do blend,
With silent whispers that extend,
Through the still waters of the mind,
Where peace and reverie unwind.

In mirrored depths, where musings lie,
Soft ripples breathe a wistful sigh,
Life's questions rolled in muted glow,
Ebb and flow as time does show.

By twilight's grace, in hues so rare,
A truth revealed in opalescent glare,
That even in the softest tones,
The heart can find it's truest home.

Dream Weaver's Sonnet

Dream weaver's touch on silken threads,
Crafts a tapestry where hope is fed,
Each stitch a story, each seam a song,
In the realm where dreamers belong.

By moonlit loom in shadows deep,
Awake the visions that angels keep,
With gentle hands and whisper light,
They mend the tears of darkest night.

Patterns emerge in softest hues,
A dance of stars, celestial muse,
Night's symphony, so softly spun,
Weaves the dawn its gentle hum.

In woven dreams, the heart takes flight,
Through realms unseen in crystal light,
Dream weaver's sonnet, pure and clear,
Whispers of love in the dreamer's ear.

Whispers Through Closed Eyes

Whispers drift on twilight's breeze,
Soft and gentle, minds they tease.
In the hush of night, dreams arise,
Through closed eyes, the soul flies.

Stars in slumber, tales unfurl,
Mystic dances, shadow swirl.
Lost in realms of silent cries,
Whispers float where deep sleep lies.

Ethereal realms, truth disguise,
Guiding light in darkened skies.
Through the veil where secrets slide,
Whispers through closed eyes abide.

Veils of Wonder

Veils of wonder, thin as mist,
Spread their magic, sunlight kissed.
In their folds, the marvels wade,
Dreams and wishes, softly played.

Through the haze, the spirits glide,
Mystic currents, verra de tide.
Ancient tales in whispers told,
Through the veils, the heart is bold.

Hushed the world, as secrets break,
Veils of wonder, souls they wake.
Where the known and unknown meet,
Wonders trace our every beat.

Half-Formed Visions

In the realm of half-light bliss,
Half-formed visions, meanings twist.
Shadows play, and shapes transform,
In the heart of twilight's storm.

Ephemeral dreams, drifting slow,
Truths and fancies, ebb and flow.
In between the day and night,
Visions born from fading light.

Glimpses of what might have been,
Half-formed worlds, both seen and unseen.
In the fringes, thoughts reside,
In those visions half-defined.

Imaginary Companions

In the vast terrain of mind,
Imaginary friends we find.
Shaped from dreams and lonely hours,
Companions born from inner towers.

Whispered secrets, laughter shared,
In their presence, none compared.
Unseen bonds that time can't sever,
Imaginary friends forever.

Through each chapter, side by side,
In the hidden world, they bide.
Though unseen by waking light,
They remain, a cherished sight.

Embroidery of the Unseen

In threads of air, the needles weave,
Tales of spirits, whispered light.
Invisible looms, they interleave,
Dim tapestries of night.

Ephemeral touch, a fleeting trace,
Patterns hidden, dusk to dawn.
Colors born from void embrace,
The fabric of the non.

Stitches fine, by wraiths unseen,
Moments lost, yet still entwined.
In the silence, softly glean,
The secrets left behind.

Unraveled dreams, in twilight caught,
A dance of shadows, subtle grace.
From darkness, with a purpose fraught,
They bloom unto the space.

Each ghostly thread, a silent hymn,
In quiet luster, softly sheen.
We grasp their essence, faint and thin,
Embroidery of the unseen.

Idylls of the Heart

In gardens hidden 'neath the chest,
Where roses bloom in crimson hue.
Echoes present, softly blessed,
A love both deep and true.

Whispered winds through leaves above,
Songs of solace, sweet repose.
In the canopy of love,
In hearts' eternal groves.

Paths of dreams we wander by,
Holding hands in twilight's cast.
Beneath the ever-changing sky,
In memories' clasp, we're fast.

Sunlight fades but still we yearn,
For idyllic days of past.
In heart's embrace, we always turn,
To moments meant to last.

Forevermore, in tender lair,
From first to lasts, our spirits part.
Yet fervently we'll cherish there,
The idylls of the heart.

Mysteries in Moonlight

Beneath the silver lunar gaze,
Mysteries whispered in the night.
The veil of stars begins to raise,
And hidden worlds take flight.

Shadows dance on silent streams,
Reflecting secrets from the sky.
In moonbeam's tender, gentle gleam,
Unraveled truths lie nigh.

Ancient whispers in the breeze,
Stories told by elm and pine.
In moonlit nights the heart believes,
In wonders so divine.

The seer's eye through twilight peers,
Unveiling threads of cosmic lore.
In mystic light dissolves the fears,
Of what lies yet in store.

Upon this stage of pearl and grey,
Eternal myths and dreams ignite.
In moon's soft glow, we find our way,
Through mysteries in moonlight.

Etheric Embrace

In realms where mortal sight may fail,
An etheric touch we find.
A tender grace beyond the veil,
That binds the heart and mind.

In invisible arms, we're clasped and kept,
A presence felt yet seen not quite.
In dreams, we walk where angels stepped,
Embraced by love's own light.

The breath of life, an unseen force,
Carries whispers, soft and clear.
Through etheric paths we course,
With spirits ever near.

In moments of the deepest peace,
A warmth surrounds, a gentle flow.
An unseen, loving force's release,
In hearts it softly glows.

So trust in bonds we cannot see,
The silent hands that interlace.
For in this life and beyond it be,
We dwell in etheric embrace.

Phantasmagoric Portraits

Shadows paint the midnight air,
Brushstrokes dance without a care.
Faces flicker, truths distort,
In the canvas dreams consort.

Lines of time, a fleeting show,
Mysteries in twilight's glow.
Colors bleed, reality bends,
In this realm where sight transcends.

Mirrors of the soul reveal,
Depths where hidden wishes steal.
Phantom lights in darkened skies,
Wandering through bygone lies.

Figures whisper tales untold,
In the twilight's gentle hold.
Every stroke a secret keeps,
In the gallery where silence weeps.

Eyes that see beyond the veil,
Catching glimpses, faint and frail.
Ephemeral, the ghosts remain,
Bound within this spectral frame.

Reverberations of Thought

Echoes in the mind's deep hall,
Whispered words that rise and fall.
Fleeting glimpses, shadows cast,
Fragments of a distant past.

Ideas drift like morning mist,
In the thoughts where dreams persist.
Every notion, bold and slight,
Flickers in the mind's twilight.

Words unsaid, emotions raw,
Reverberate through minds in awe.
In the silence, wisdom grows,
From the depths where insight flows.

Silent murmurs, loud and clear,
Speak of truths we hold most dear.
In our hearts, the thoughts align,
Weaving tales of the divine.

Within the echo's soft embrace,
Find the thoughts we can't erase.
Melodies of mental threads,
Where reflection gently treads.

Silhouettes of Serenity

Quiet scenes where calm resides,
In the heart where peace abides.
Silent whispers, gentle streams,
Flow within our tranquil dreams.

Nature's song in muted grace,
Softly kissing time and space.
Shadows dance with light's caress,
In a world of calm finesse.

Evening's veil of twilight cast,
Bringing peace that holds us fast.
Crickets' chorus, night's refrain,
Serenades the soul in gain.

Mountains stand in silent might,
Guardians of the fading light.
In their shadows, we find rest,
In the quiet, feeling blessed.

In the stillness, hearts entwine,
With serenity's design.
Moments pass but never fade,
In this calm, we're gently swayed.

A Dance with Dreams

In the night where dreams take flight,
Hearts alight in moon's soft light.
Steps of wonder, rhythms clear,
Waltz in realms both far and near.

Visions rise in slumber's grace,
Ephemeral in time and space.
Twining threads of hope and fear,
Tales untold but close, so dear.

Stars align in silv'ry dance,
Guiding us through dream's expanse.
In the shadows, light reveals,
Hidden truths our spirit feels.

Mystic paths through twilight fields,
Every dream a secret yields.
Dancing with the night's embrace,
Tracing out our souls' own face.

Morning comes, a gentle sweep,
Whispers of the dreams we keep.
In our hearts, the dance persists,
In the realm where slumber twists.

Dreamscapes Unveiled

In realms where visions brightly flow,
Unseen by weary, waking eye.
Colors blend in grand tableau,
Dimensions shift as you soar high.

Whispers of a world unknown,
Where moonlight dances 'cross the streams.
Mountains rise to kiss the sky,
A wondrous tapestry of dreams.

Stars like jewels adorn the night,
Soft winds weave through fields of gold.
Here, where heart and mind take flight,
Stories of the soul are told.

Embrace the beauty, pure and wild,
A landscape painted by desire.
In dreamscapes free, forever child,
To realms where hopes and thoughts aspire.

Awake, yet longing to return,
To lands where fantasy unveiled.
A world where endless wonders yearn,
And every captured breath exhaled.

Melancholy Murmurs

Through shadows deep and voices low,
The heart recalls what once it knew.
A whispered tale in moonlit glow,
Of days long past and love so true.

The autumn leaves in hues of rust,
They fall like remnants of a dream.
The echoes fade into the dust,
A silent, solitary theme.

The river's song, a mournful tune,
Reflects the sky's translucent grey.
Beneath the sorrow of the moon,
The memories of yesterdays.

In twilight's gentle, somber hue,
The soul does wander, lost in time.
A journey through the faint and few,
Of moments held in wistful rhyme.

Yet through the tears of night alone,
A glimmer of the dawn draws near.
For in the melancholic tone,
There stirs a hope beyond the tear.

Reflections in the Twilight

At day's end, as shadows grow long,
In twilight's tender, fading light.
The heart hums to an ancient song,
A soft embrace of coming night.

The world is bathed in amber hue,
As stars emerge in velvet sky.
Minds drift to places they once knew,
A time when dreams could freely fly.

Whispering winds through branches weave,
The secrets of the night are told.
In silence, souls begin to grieve,
For tales that time will never hold.

Mirrors of the past we see,
In twilight's soft, reflective glow.
Moments glisten, fleetingly,
In memory's gentle undertow.

The night invites a tranquil peace,
As daylight bids its last adieu.
In twilight's calm, reflections cease,
And hearts renew with dreams anew.

Illusions of the Mind

In labyrinths of thought concealed,
Where reason meets a shifting shade.
The borders of the mind revealed,
In patterns dark and life portrayed.

A dance of phantoms, fleeting, bright,
In corridors of endless hue.
Illusions born of primal light,
Yet truths that seem forever true.

The echoes of the heart's refrain,
Through canyons deep and shadows wide.
A whispered song of joy and pain,
Where consciousness and dreams collide.

In mirrors of the mind's delight,
Reflections twist and sway in time.
An endless play of dark and light,
A haunting, enigmatic rhyme.

Seek not the answers clear and plain,
In realms where thought and vision blend.
For in the mind's surreal domain,
Illusions form and never end.

Of Sleep and Soft Dreams

In the hush of night's embrace,
Whispers weave a tender lace,
Stars above begin to gleam,
Guiding us to realms unseen.

Softly falls the velvet night,
Cradling us in gentle light,
Wonders in the silence grow,
As the moon begins to glow.

Eyes grow heavy, breath is slow,
In the quiet shadows flow,
In this boundless realm, we soar,
Through the twilight's open door.

Sweet the scent of dreams, a sigh,
As we drift neath starry sky,
Bound by threads of sleep's sweet song,
In this place, we do belong.

Daydream Lullabies

Golden sunlight softly weaves,
Through the canopy of leaves,
Whispered dreams in daylight's grasp,
As the breeze holds truths to clasp.

Silent notes of unseen breeze,
Layered with the song of trees,
Patterns form as shadows play,
Echoes of a wistful day.

Soft is the dream that finds my mind,
In the hues of day refined,
Wandering through fields of thought,
With each glimmer, more is caught.

Time is still, yet dreams do flow,
In this realm, no bounds we know,
Day awakens night's soft flings,
And the heart, content, it sings.

Mirrored in the Still Waters

Upon the lake, the silence spread,
In tranquil waves, reflections fed,
Mirror of the world unseen,
In the calm, the soft serene.

Ripples trace the quiet night,
Drawing dreams in liquid light,
Whispers of the sky descend,
In the stillness, they suspend.

Moonlight kisses on the glass,
Eternal moment, time does pass,
In this mirror, secrets keep,
Lulled by waters, breathe in deep.

Softly bade by wind's soft sighs,
Stars reflected in our eyes,
Dreams are woven, while we gaze,
In this world of water's maze.

Tales from Twilight Hues

Twilight wraps the earth in blue,
Softened light, a different view,
Whispers of the day resign,
In the twilight's gentle sign.

Colors blend in evening's veil,
Nature spins a timeless tale,
Between the dusk and dawning light,
Stories carried through the night.

Here the shadows start to sway,
Hinting at another day,
Twilight's hues, a solace find,
In the gentle, winding mind.

Stars begin their solemn rise,
In the cradle of the skies,
Tales from twilight softly spun,
Resting 'neath the setting sun.

Spherical Silences

In the stillness of the night,
Whispers round a silken sphere,
Silent echoes take their flight,
From the shadows, ghosts appear.

Moonlight weaves a silver ring,
Circles softly, seeking peace,
In this dance where spirits sing,
Timeless moments find release.

Stars converse in muted rhyme,
Orb of dreams, our thoughts align,
Bound by threads of spaceless time,
In the silence, worlds entwine.

Mirrored Reveries

Glass reflections tell a tale,
Of dreams held in crystal sighs,
Where our hearts and hands set sail,
In the place where silence lies.

Mystic realms within the glass,
Mirrored whispers call our name,
Future shadows, echoes past,
Each a fragment of the same.

Twilight's gaze through pane so clear,
Mirrored selves in search of truth,
In the mist, a vision near,
Age and innocence of youth.

Dreamscapes of the Soul

Drift where visions paint the sky,
Hues of spirit, born in light,
Through the realms where whispers sigh,
In the canvas of the night.

Wander shadows of the mind,
Speak in colors, bright and bold,
Stories in the waves we find,
Tales of love and dreams retold.

Journey far from time's embrace,
In the heart's eternal scroll,
Trace the lines upon our face,
In the dreamscapes of the soul.

Whispers in the Twilight

Shadows fall as daylight fades,
Softly blending night's first breath,
In the twilight's gentle shades,
Murmurs rise from realms beneath.

Crickets hum a dusk-lit tune,
Night's first whisper greets the stars,
Underneath the silver moon,
Dreams unfold in whispering bars.

Silent winds weave lullabies,
In the twilight's hush so deep,
Whispers sing as daylight dies,
In this world where secrets sleep.

Glimpses of the Infinite

Stars sprinkle the indigo sky,
Each one a story untold,
In a vast and silent dance,
Eternal secrets unfold.

Waves whisper to the shore,
Tales from the deep blue,
In every crest and trough,
Infinite glimpses accrue.

Mountains touch the heavens,
Their peaks kissed by the sun,
In their solemn embrace,
Infinity has begun.

In the murmur of the wind,
A symphony of old,
Timeless notes of nature,
In whispers bright and bold.

Glimpses of the infinite,
In every beat of time,
Echoes of the cosmos,
In existence so sublime.

Whimsy in the Quiet Hours

Moonlight bathes the sleeping town,
Casting shadows long,
In the stillness of the night,
Echoes a soft, sweet song.

The trees sway to a tune,
Only the wind can hear,
In the quiet, whispers play,
Melodies soft and clear.

The owl softly hoots above,
A guardian of the night,
Lending to the serenity,
With eyes so round and bright.

Footsteps echo on cobblestones,
A dance nobody sees,
Whimsy in the quiet hours,
Carried on a gentle breeze.

Dreams weave through the silence,
Where fantasies take flight,
In the hush of the dark,
Lies the magic of the night.

Visions Beyond the Veil

Mist rolls over the hollow,
Cloaking the world in grey,
In its quiet embrace,
Old spirits come to play.

Shadows cast on forgotten walls,
Whispering tales untold,
In the twilight's tender grasp,
Mysteries unfold.

The veil of night descends,
Curtains of dusk unfurl,
Visions dance in the dark,
In an otherworldly swirl.

Eyes that search the heavens,
Glimpse galaxies unknown,
In the vast, eternal sky,
Dreams have brightly shone.

Beyond the edge of sight,
Lies a world unseen,
In the heart of darkness,
Visions gleam and glean.

Flights of Fancy

On wings of pure imagination,
We soar above the plain,
In realms of whimsical fancy,
Where dreams break every chain.

Unicorns dance in moonlight,
Fairies touch the sky,
In forests made of stardust,
Where earthly bounds can't tie.

Castles float in the ether,
Built of clouds and dreams,
On each turret gleams a hope,
In the sunlight's beams.

Dragons guard the treasure,
Of stories yet untold,
In caverns bright with wonder,
Lies magic to behold.

In flights of purest fancy,
The soul finds its own wings,
Touched by the breath of freedom,
In the heart, joy sings.

Whispers in Daydreams

Beneath a sky of endless blue,
Where golden sunrays softly gleam,
I close my eyes to wander through,
The whispers woven in my dream.

Glimpses of a land unknown,
Where time and space in silence meet,
A world where seeds of magic sown,
Bloom in fields of bright deceit.

Voices call from shadow's edge,
Gently luring my heart's flight,
Lingering just beyond the hedge,
Where twilight blends with dawn's light.

Clouds of thought billow and sway,
In a dance of pure delight,
Within this dreamscape I will stay,
While whispers weave the endless night.

From slumber's grasp I softly wake,
To find the day is not a dream,
For hidden truths like oceans break,
In whispers through the daylight beam.

Echoes of Enchantment

Waves of moonlight gently kiss,
The surface of an enchanted lake,
Where ancient trees in silent bliss,
Guard secrets time could never take.

Mystic beings softly tread,
On paths of silver, shadows cast,
In whispers old and stories said,
They echo legends from the past.

Beneath the canopy of stars,
In twilight's tender, fleeting grace,
A symphony without guitars,
Plays melodies of time and space.

Eons fold in moments brief,
As whispers blend with night's embrace,
Spelling out belief and grief,
In every contour of this place.

When dawn's first light begins to creep,
The echoes fade into the air,
Leaving imprints in the deep,
Of something timeless, pure, and rare.

Serenade of Solitude

In the hollow of the night,
Where silence sings a haunting tune,
Lonely shadows greet the light,
Of distant stars and pale moon.

Each note a sigh, a wistful plea,
From hearts that yearn but cannot find,
A sense of peace or harmony,
Within the solitude consigned.

Winds that whisper through the pines,
Carry tales of love forlorn,
Humming through the quiet lines,
Of nights that stretch till early morn.

In every breath the world takes,
An echo lingers, soft and clear,
A serenade that humbly wakes,
The tender ache of being near.

Yet within this void so vast,
There lies a beauty, pure and true,
Moments of a quiet past,
Compose a serenade for you.

Canvas of Imagined Realms

Upon a canvas wide and grand,
I paint with dreams of distant lands,
Where mountains rise and oceans stand,
In harmony with shifting sands.

Colors blend in vibrant streaks,
Crafting worlds where wonder lies,
Forests where the silence speaks,
To creatures born of star-filled skies.

Castles touch the heavens high,
In realms where magic rules the day,
Dragons soar and phoenix fly,
Through twilight's ever-radiant ray.

Every stroke a story casts,
Drawing life from thought's deep well,
Imagined realms from futures past,
Where hopes and endless mysteries dwell.

When the final stroke is laid,
And colors rest in calm repose,
The canvas of my dreams displayed,
A vital world in daylight's glow.

Ode to Slumber Songs

The night descends, a silken shroud,
Soft whispers weave a lullaby.
Stars awaken, gleaming proud,
As dreams begin their gentle sigh.

Pillows cradling thoughts of light,
A moonlit dance on sheets of white.
Eyes close gently, veiling sight,
In slumber's arms, the heart is tight.

Murmurs float on twilight air,
A world within, where none compare.
Silent echoes, dark and fair,
In sleep's domain, we find repair.

Underneath the ebon sky,
Midnight's hymn will softly ply.
From dusk till dawn, a sweet reply,
To every wisp of dream we try.

When morning rays the night displace,
Awake, refreshed by night's embrace.
Yet still we crave that tender space,
Where slumber songs our souls retrace.

Echoes in the Aether

Through the void, a whisper calls,
In silent waves, the message falls.
Unseen threads within the walls,
Of space and time, the echo sprawls.

Where shadows blend in cosmic dust,
And stars ignite with ancient lust.
Child of silence, in you we trust,
To carry forth and ne'er combust.

Galactic winds, a subtle breeze,
Whispers through the endless seas.
Time and space begin to freeze,
In this suspended state of ease.

Across the void, the echoes play,
Through night and dark and breaking day.
A symphony in disarray,
Yet perfect in its own array.

The aether hums a distant tone,
A song for wanderers alone.
In echoes, find the world unknown,
A universe that once was shown.

Contours of Lucidity

In lucid dreams, the scenes unfold,
A tapestry of stories told.
Each thread of light, a tale of gold,
Within the mind, the secret hold.

Colors breathe and shadows melt,
In states of waking, never felt.
A realm where every truth is dealt,
By contours of the thoughts we've smelt.

Boundaries blur and walls dissolve,
In lucid moments, we evolve.
Mysteries of life, we solve,
As waking's chains we swift absolve.

From light to dark, the spectrum bends,
A lucid dance that never ends.
In sleep, the dreaming self defends,
The line 'twixt worlds that mind intends.

When waking comes and lucids fade,
The dreams retreat in night's parade.
Yet traces of their light will wade,
In minds where contours lucid stayed.

Mirage of Moments

Moments fleeting, dusk to dawn,
Ephemeral as a whispered yawn.
In the blink of eye, they're gone,
As time's relentless river's drawn.

Mirages of time we seek,
In memories, we hear them speak.
Phantoms of the past we peek,
In every fleeting mystique streak.

Shade of joy and hue of sorrow,
Silent echoes of tomorrow.
Temporality we borrow,
In moments we refine and sorrow.

Glimpses of what could have been,
In mirage, we find the scene.
A dance of seconds, all unseen,
Time's illusion, lean and keen.

When time eludes and moments part,
Mirages remain a subtle art.
In dreams and thoughts, they rechart,
The fleeting pulse within the heart.

Soul's Nocturnal Wanderings

In the hush of twilight's gleam,
Spirits wander, chasing dreams.
Under moon's soft silver lace,
They find solace, traces of grace.

Silent forests, shadows deep,
Whisper tales that secrets keep.
Stars above, like ancient lore,
Guide the souls to distant shore.

Wind's caress, a ghostly kiss,
Echoes of forgotten bliss.
Mountains tall and valleys wide,
Dreams and whispers coincide.

Through the veil of midnight air,
Souls embrace a world so rare.
Mystic paths they tread once more,
In the heart of night's allure.

Celestial dance on starlit sea,
Boundless realms where spirits flee.
By dawn's light, they gently fade,
In the day's curtain, dreams are made.

Veil of Sleep's Embrace

Softly fades the waning light,
As the stars ignite the night.
In their glow, a tender trace,
Of the veil of sleep's embrace.

Whispers of the twilight breeze,
Gentle lull that hearts appease.
Dreams unfold with quiet grace,
Held within this tranquil space.

Moonlit paths and silver streams,
Guiding souls through gentle dreams.
With each breath, the night consumes,
All that daylight's glare assumes.

Silent world in hues of gray,
Nighttime weaves its gentle sway.
Wrapped in sleep's warm tender fold,
Wonders in the dark unfold.

As dawn's light begins to rise,
Night's embrace, a soft disguise.
Memories of dreams remain,
Carried on the morning's train.

Among Illuminated Petals

Underneath the moon's soft glow,
Petals shine and roses grow.
In the garden, hearts elate,
Bright with dreams they cultivate.

Wandering through fragrant blooms,
Magic in the evening looms.
Whispers of the flowers' hue,
Under stars of night's debut.

Petals kissed by evening's dew,
In their light, a world anew.
Colors dance in twilight's reign,
Beauty found in night's sweet pain.

Breezes weave a lullaby,
Soft and gentle, shadows fly.
In the hush of nature's sleep,
Secrets in the flowers keep.

By the dawn, the petals wake,
From the dream that night did make.
Illuminated, they reveal,
Moments that the night could steal.

Breath of Dreamy Waves

When the ocean whispers faint,
Songs of night with soft restraint.
Waves that sigh and breezes play,
In the dusk of end-of-day.

Moonlit tides with gentle sway,
Dreams like shadows drift away.
On the crest of waters deep,
Echoes rise from tranquil sleep.

Silver threads through midnight's core,
Weave the dreams on sandy shore.
Breath of waves, a tender lull,
Soothes the mind and heart's annul.

In the rhythm, lost in time,
Dreams unfold in ocean's rhyme.
Depths of blue and skies that weep,
Hold the secrets waters keep.

As the morning light appears,
Dreams recede with fading fears.
Breath of waves, a tender grace,
Leaves the night without a trace.

In the Garden of Unseen Thoughts

In the garden of unseen thoughts,
Where dreams are gently caught.
Whispers of hope softly breeze,
Through the shade of silent trees.

Petals of ideas start to bloom,
In the quiet, sacred room.
Unshed tears water the ground,
Where lost emotions can be found.

Paths of wonder intertwine,
Leading hearts to places divine.
The mind's eye begins to see,
What is and what could be.

Echoes of unspoken words,
Fly like free and gentle birds.
In this tranquil mind retreat,
Imaginations' worlds do meet.

Beneath the canopy of thought,
Love and fears are deftly wrought.
In the garden's hidden spin,
The soul's true journey will begin.

Wanderlust of the Unconscious

In the wanderlust of sleep,
Secrets buried dark and deep.
Tales of yore and what's to come,
Blend in mind's ephemeral hum.

Each dream a vivid place,
With no time, nor defined space.
Dancing shadows weave and wind,
Through the corridors of mind.

Beyond the waking world's edge,
Lies a truth to softly pledge.
In the quiet of the night,
Unseen worlds come to light.

Vistas painted with pure thought,
Journeys that can't be bought.
Hopeless, hopeful tales entwine,
In the unconscious' grand design.

Lost within the endless maze,
Of twilight's boundless haze.
The spirit's travels evermore,
Through an ever-open door.

Curtains of Midnight Whispers

Curtains of whispered night,
Drawn against the flickered light.
Shadows dance in hidden realms,
Quiet thoughts at midnight helms.

Underneath the moon's soft gaze,
Mysteries of night amaze.
Silent voices call out low,
Cloaked in darkness' gentle glow.

Beneath the star-kissed sky,
Dreams and secrets softly lie.
Whispered words take shape and form,
In the quiet midnight storm.

Memories and future blend,
In the night where whispers send.
Thoughts astray in mellow streams,
Glide on whispers of moonbeams.

Curtains lift, revealing dreams,
Crafted by night's subtle schemes.
Each whisper a story spun,
Under midnight, softly begun.

In the Realm of Soft Illusions

In the realm of soft illusions,
Truth and dream make sweet confusions.
Visions float like drifting mist,
On a night by moonlight kissed.

In the haze, the mind will wander,
Through each whisper, softly ponder.
Mirrored lakes and twilight glows,
Blend in fluid, gentle flows.

Magic in each glance perceived,
By the heart that's unreceived.
Oceans of forgotten streams,
Stir the depths of wandering dreams.

Borders fade and blur the lines,
Between what's real and what confines.
Light and shadow gently play,
In the soft, illusioned sway.

In this realm where thoughts are free,
Truth in dream is what we see.
Softly, softly we are led,
Through illusions in our head.

When Stars Begin to Sing

In the quiet of the night,
Where whispers softly cling,
Dreams take their flight,
When stars begin to sing.

Across the sky they dance,
With a melody so rare,
A cosmic, bright romance,
Lights the midnight air.

Galaxies hum along,
In a universal choir,
Every note a perfect song,
Raising spirits higher.

The moon lends its gentle glow,
To the harmonic ring,
In the nocturnal show,
When stars begin to sing.

Every heart and soul,
Feels the celestial swing,
Life becomes whole,
When stars begin to sing.

Enchanted Interludes

Beneath the twilight's veil,
A magic softly weaves,
Stories old and frail,
In enchanted interludes' leaves.

Whispers of time gone by,
In shadows softly play,
Under a moonlit sky,
They greet the break of day.

Mystic tales unfold,
In every twilight hue,
With secrets yet untold,
In shades of silver blue.

In that fleeting pause,
Where day and night converge,
Life escapes its claws,
In enchanted interludes, we surge.

Awake, the world, anew,
From the night's embrace,
In every morning dew,
Magic leaves its trace.

The Realm of Fluttering Ideas

In the quiet of the mind,
Thoughts take their wings,
Every treasure you will find,
In the realm of fluttering ideas, it sings.

Dreams and visions blend,
With colors vivid, bright,
Endless paths they send,
To our boundless inner sight.

Concepts twirl and spin,
In whimsical delight,
A world created within,
Bursting into light.

Each notion a spark,
In a celestial dance,
A journey we embark,
With imagination's trance.

In the mind's serene play,
Where creativity resides,
Fluttering ideas lay,
In the realm where freedom abides.

Between Waking and Dreaming

In the twilight's gentle hold,
Where day meets the night,
Stories softly unfold,
In the between's light.

Echoes of the waking world,
Mingle with dreams untamed,
In this place, magic swirled,
Imagination unclaimed.

Time unfolds a quilt,
Of shadows and gleams,
Moments gently built,
Between waking and dreams.

Here, the heart finds peace,
In quiet, serene theme,
Worries gently cease,
In the realm of the in-between.

As night slowly ascends,
And day gracefully wanes,
The mystical blend,
Between waking and dreaming remains.

Reflections in Silver Streams

In the hush of twilight's gleams,
Ripples carry water's dreams.
Silver whispers paint the night,
Mirrors gleam in moon's soft light.

Time stands still on river's edge,
Quiet flows that hush and pledge.
Every wave a whispered song,
Gentle currents drift along.

Trees bend low to softly kiss,
Where reflections meet in bliss.
Shadows dance on silver tides,
Nature's secrets there confide.

Moonbeams cast a gentle glow,
Softly guiding where to go.
Mysteries in the water's seam,
Found in silver, soft and serene.

Reflections merge with midnight hues,
In perfect calm, no fear ensues.
In the silver streams, we find,
Echoes of a tranquil mind.

Delicate Daydreams

Whispers in the quiet air,
Soft dreams carried everywhere.
Gentle thoughts like feather's fall,
Delicate, they weave and call.

Sunlight through the leafy shade,
Unspoken wishes gently laid.
As the day begins to dance,
In daydreams, we find our chance.

Clouds of cotton, skies of blue,
Morning's rays in golden hue.
In the stillness, minds can drift,
Daydreams rise and spirits lift.

Wandering through a canvas white,
Imagination takes its flight.
Every moment, freshly spun,
In the daylight, dreams begun.

Softly painted, skies serene,
In delicate daydreams, scenes.
Infinite, our minds can trace,
In daydreams, a tender grace.

When Clouds Spell Stories

Whispers in the azure sea,
Clouds inventing mystery.
Shapes that twist, then disappear,
Stories form and reappear.

Every drift a tale unfurls,
Legends of the sky in swirls.
In the boundless, endless height,
Clouds recount the day and night.

Figures in the fleeting mist,
Moments that the sun has kissed.
Every puff and wisp reveal,
Tales the heavens can't conceal.

Dancing in the morning glow,
Words in clouds begin to flow.
Narratives of silent flight,
Mysteries in pure daylight.

High above where dreams unfold,
Stories in the sky are told.
In clouds that spell and softly part,
Secrets whispered from the heart.

Dancing with Shadows

In the twilight's tender glow,
Shadows rise and ebb and flow.
Silent steps on evening's stage,
Dancing free from time and age.

Every movement, smooth and sleek,
Mysteries these forms bespeak.
Shapes that sway with silent grace,
In the dusk, they find their place.

Night entwines with shadows' dance,
Darkness leads the quiet trance.
Partners in the dimming light,
Bound in rhythm, pure and tight.

Softly, shadows intertwine,
Spirits in the evening's spine.
Fluid motions, undefined,
In the darkness, freedom finds.

In the night, a silent song,
Shadows dance and glide along.
Echoes of the day's sweet end,
In the dark, their dances blend.

Enigma of the Soul

In depths of night where shadows play,
A silent whisper seeks its way,
Unseen threads that webs entwine,
Bind the heart to realms divine.

Mysteries linger, veiled in dark,
In dreams, they leave their subtle mark,
A soul's enigma, pure and vast,
Echoes of a distant past.

Nebulous realms of thought and grace,
A mirror reflects an unknown face,
Journey inward, seek to find,
Hidden truths within the mind.

Celestial light, a lantern guide,
Through twilight whispers, hearts confide,
An inner sanctum, secrets told,
In shadows of the soul, unfold.

Beyond the finite, souls will soar,
To realms where mysteries adore,
In search of timeless, endless whole,
Lies the enigma of the soul.

Veils of Tranquility

Softly, softly, whispers breeze,
Among the leaves of ancient trees,
Cradled in a quiet grove,
These are places hearts do rove.

Whispers of the morning dew,
Hold the secrets pure and true,
Tranquil lakes in mirrored glow,
Gentle waves and currents flow.

Beneath the sky, serene and wide,
Dreams like rivers, gently glide,
A world at peace, a soul at rest,
In tranquil veils, we are blest.

Stillness wraps in tender fold,
Stories of the earth unfold,
Nature's hymn, a serene call,
In tranquil veils, we find all.

Within these veils, a heart does lie,
Eternal calm under the sky,
Tranquility in every breath,
A gentle dance with life and death.

Wandering in the Clouds

Across the sky, the canvas vast,
With dreamy hues that fade so fast,
We wander through the airy rise,
Among the clouds, we cast our eyes.

Floating in the ether blue,
With every breeze, a dance we do,
Shapes and forms in endless scroll,
Celestial tales that lift the soul.

Solitude in fluffy white,
A journey far from day to night,
Cloudscapes morph in silent grace,
A wandering in boundless space.

Gliding slow through heavens wide,
With misty dreams as our guide,
Infinite in form and hue,
A skyward path, forever new.

Above the world, where moments cease,
We drift in realms of pure release,
In clouds' embrace, our spirits free,
We find an endless reverie.

Veins of Imagination

Within the mind, a river flows,
Through veins of thought, where wonder grows,
Imagination's boundless stream,
Shapes the world in vivid dream.

A canvas blank, with colors bright,
Dreams take flight in boundless light,
From ink of stars, the sky unfolds,
Stories vast and yet untold.

Through corridors of silent muse,
Where shadows dance, and lights diffuse,
In every heart's secluded hall,
Shimmers of the endless call.

Worlds are spun on fantasy's thread,
Ideas with wings, by visions led,
In veins of mind, life's essence sings,
Imagination's fervent springs.

Crafting worlds with thought's embrace,
A tapestry of time and space,
In every vein, creation flows,
In endless dreams, imagination grows.

Veil of Ethereal Thoughts

In the quiet of twilight, whispers take flight,
Beneath the canopy of stars, dreams ignite.
Veils of thoughts, so tender and frail,
Drift on moonbeams, where secrets sail.

The winds of change, they softly blow,
Through fields of memory, where shadows glow.
In the hush of night, hearts find their peace,
Moments of stillness, where worries cease.

Each thought a feather, light and free,
Carried by whispers from a hidden sea.
In ethereal dance, they weave and wind,
In the corners of the mind, beauty to find.

Stars gaze down with silent grace,
As time slows in this sacred place.
Veil of thoughts, translucent and bright,
Guides the soul through the gentle night.

In dreams we wander, far and near,
Through the veil of thoughts, so crystal clear.
In the silence of night, hearts interlace,
Finding solace in that timeless space.

Contours of a Dreamscape

In the realm where shadows play,
Contours of dreams in soft array.
Mountains rise and rivers wind,
Echoes of a world left behind.

Colors blend in twilight's gleam,
Edges blurred in a waking dream.
Footsteps echo, soft and clear,
Guiding onward, far and near.

Whispering winds, a gentle call,
Through forests deep and caverns tall.
In this landscape, visions roam,
Finding whispers, a place called home.

Stars align in cosmic dance,
Casting light on happenstance.
Threads of wonder, weaving tight,
In the tapestry of night.

At dawn's first light, visions fade,
Yet within the heart, they're laid.
Contours of a dreamscape vast,
In memories, forever cast.

The Place of Forgotten Myth

In the shadow of ancient trees,
Whispers of forgotten breeze.
Legends told in voices low,
Where the river of time does flow.

Dragons slept 'neath moonlit skies,
Giants walked, where hills now lie.
Mermaids sang in oceans deep,
In dreams, their secrets keep.

Temples grand, now lost in sand,
Magic ruled this timeless land.
In the ruins, echoes play,
Of a time that slipped away.

Mysteries in the silent night,
Stars that guided heroes' flight.
In this place, where stories rest,
Lost mythologies, the universe's quest.

Though the myths may fade and fall,
In hearts, they still stand tall.
In the place of forgotten rhyme,
Legends live beyond all time.

Silent Conversations

In the quiet of a moonlit night,
Words unspoken take their flight.
Eyes that meet, souls that touch,
Silent conversations mean so much.

Beneath the stars, hearts converse,
In a language, the universe.
Softly spoken, without sound,
In silence, love is found.

Glimmers of understanding gleam,
In the spaces in between.
Whispers of the soul align,
In the quiet moments, hearts entwine.

Through the hush, emotions blend,
In the silence, hearts transcend.
Shared in quiet, without speech,
Lessons only stillness can teach.

In the silence, truth is laid,
Words unspoken, but conveyed.
Conversing in the quiet night,
In silence, souls take flight.

Murmurs of Forgotten Time

In the twilight's tender glow,
Whispers of the past arise,
Echoes of a time long gone,
Beneath the starlit skies.

Ancient tales of joy and woe,
Flow through the evening air,
Haunting murmurs of forgotten time,
In memories' soft repair.

Leaves rustle with secrets old,
Revealing history's veil,
As shadows dance in whispered tones,
Where fading echoes trail.

Steps we've traced in yesteryears,
Now linger in the dusk,
Time's gentle hand erases all,
Leaving just a faint musk.

The silent moon guards the night,
With stories old and grand,
Murmurs of forgotten time,
Rest on this ancient land.

Illuminated Horizons

Sunrise paints the sky anew,
With hues of gold and rose,
The horizon cradles dreams,
Where endless journey flows.

Mountains kiss the morning light,
Their peaks aglow with fire,
Illuminating horizons,
As hearts and hopes aspire.

The world bathes in radiant beams,
Nature's canvas, bright and vast,
Guided by the dawn's embrace,
Future steps so bravely cast.

Winds of change beckon near,
With whispers soft and mild,
Inviting souls to venture forth,
With spirits free and wild.

Beneath the boundless, open sky,
Where dreams and earth align,
Illuminated horizons gleam,
In the morning's grand design.

Fleeting Illusions

Ephemeral dreams weave through night,
Like shadows through the light,
Fleeting whispers, almost real,
Dancing just out of sight.

Mirages flicker in the mind,
Promises so pure,
Yet vanish with the morning sun,
As dawn's light starts to lure.

Hopes that bloom then fade away,
Like echoes of a song,
Chasing phantoms in the dark,
Where fleeting dreams belong.

The moon reflects our deepest fears,
And secrets of the heart,
Illusions weave their fragile spell,
Only to fall apart.

Delicate as morning dew,
Dispersed by first sunlight,
Fleeting illusions fade to naught,
In the clarity of night.

Ode to the Sleepwalkers

In the silence of the night,
Their footsteps soundless fall,
Traversing dreams and shadows vast,
In a world known to all.

Eyes closed yet visions clear,
As moonlight guides their way,
Sleepwalkers drift o'er whispered paths,
To unseen realms they stray.

Unbound by day's pure logic,
They glide through mystic air,
Weaving tales of twilight's lore,
With an effortless, calm flair.

Between the realms of dreams and waking,
They silently reside,
Guardians of the night's deep thoughts,
On starlit winds they glide.

Ode to the sleepwalkers,
Lost in nocturnal trance,
In the dance of dreams and night,
Where shadows softly prance.

A Canvas of Pure Fantasies

Brush strokes of dreams on silent skies,
Whispers of tales where mystery lies.
Colors of wonder in twilight's embrace,
A realm of pure fantasies we chase.

Stars twinkle secrets in the night,
Moonlight dances, soft and bright.
In this world, our hearts take flight,
Imagination's wings, boundless in height.

Mountains hum forgotten songs,
Rivers murmur tales where time belongs.
In every shadow, a secret throng,
A canvas painted where dreams belong.

Through the mist of endless gleams,
Chasing shadows of our dreams.
Drawing lines on fate's grand themes,
Creating worlds by starlit streams.

In this kingdom of ethereal ties,
We blend reality with the skies.
Lost in a canvas where fantasy lies,
A masterpiece before our eyes.

Moments in Ethereal Hues

Dawn breaks softly in a whispering glow,
Pastel hues in morning's flow.
A symphony of light, colors anew,
Moments in ethereal hues come through.

Sunlight dances on dew-kissed leaves,
Nature's canvas, the world perceives.
Each moment captured, time's reprieve,
In ethereal hues, our hearts believe.

Shadows stretch in the afternoon's sway,
Golden hues paint the day.
In this fleeting light, we find our way,
Moments eternal, yet bound to decay.

Twilight descends with purples and blues,
Stars awaken in the cosmic muse.
Night's gentle embrace, softly ensues,
A tapestry woven in ethereal hues.

In this dance of light and shade,
Each hue, a memory fervently laid.
Moments slip through, never afraid,
Ethereal in essence, yet fatefully made.

Veins of Wandering Thoughts

Through labyrinths of a restless mind,
Wanderings leave the mundane behind.
Thoughts meander, delicately aligned,
In veins of dreams, where paths unwind.

Echoes of whispers, silent yet clear,
Navigating realms both far and near.
Thoughts flow in streams, free from fear,
In wandering's embrace, everything dear.

Star-lit dreams in a nocturnal flight,
Veins pulse with wonder, in endless night.
Every shadow a story, every gleam a light,
Thoughts unravel in the twilight's sight.

Echoes of time in currents wide,
Veins of thought, an endless tide.
Through realms obscure, we gently glide,
In wandering thoughts, eternally tied.

Beyond the horizon thought traverses,
In each mind, a universe immerses.
Wandering thoughts in silent verses,
Veins of the soul, where life converses.

Captured Light in Shadows

In shadows deep, light softly plays,
Chasing away the nocturnal haze.
A dance of contrasts where dreams stay,
Captured light in shadows' safe embrace.

Reflections in the moon's soft glow,
Eastward winds whisper low.
In these shadows, secrets flow,
Light captured where night thoughts grow.

Silhouettes of dreams, stark and bright,
Dancing whispers through the night.
In every shadow, there's a sight,
Captured light, a moonlit flight.

Darkness hues morning's trace,
In shadows, light finds its place.
A symphony of night's soft grace,
Light and dark in a tender embrace.

In the quiet of the evening's sweep,
Within shadows, secrets sleep.
Light captured in memory's keep,
A testament to the darkness deep.

Touched by Silent Winds

In whispers of the evening hue,
A breeze does softly sway the trees,
Through shadows cast in twilight's blue,
A song of calm in nature's ease.

It dances through the amber field,
Untouched by time, by toil, by care,
A gentle kiss on dreams concealed,
Swathed in the breath of autumn air.

Underneath the silent moon,
It courses over hidden streams,
Carrying secrets in its tune,
Waking the dormant, hushed dreams.

The world in hushed reverence,
Awaits the touch of winds once more,
Silent as a lover's silence,
Soft as whispers from the shore.

With every gust, tales intertwine,
With past and present, yet unseen,
A symphony so pure, divine,
Touched by silent winds, serene.

Visions in Lavender Light

In lavender light where day and night blend,
Dreams take flight in hues so tender,
Whispers of twilight softly descend,
Painting the sky with grace and splendor.

Petals glow in the dusk's embrace,
Gardens bloom in twilight's song,
Every hue finds its sacred place,
In this world where shadows belong.

The twilight veil is mystery's friend,
Concealing secrets in its thread,
Each star that twinkles knows no end,
In realms where visions are quietly spread.

Moonlight dances on rivers' glow,
Guiding night through lavender mist,
Every path it gently shows,
Leading hearts by dreams kissed.

In the glow of twilight's gleam,
Reality and dreams converge,
Within that soft, lavender beam,
Visions in light gently merge.

Uncharted Realms

Through mists of myths and shadows' play,
Lies realms untouched, where dreams reside,
Charts unseen guide one's way,
To lands where endless wonders hide.

Tales of old in whispers told,
Speak of giants, fairies, and knights,
Where mysteries unfold,
Underneath the starlit nights.

Mountains soar to skies unknown,
Forests deep with secrets keep,
Rivers flow with songs they've sown,
In realms where ancient beings sleep.

Castles in the clouds afloat,
Kingdoms in the depths below,
Through uncharted paths we dote,
On yet undiscovered glow.

In thoughts and dreams, we traverse,
These lands that imagination seals,
Exploring the vast universe,
In the heart, what wonder reveals.

The Muse's Hourglass

Time trickles through the muse's glass,
Each grain a drop of infinite mind,
Moments captured as they pass,
Creating worlds in words confined.

Wisdom hidden in fleeting sand,
Stories whispered in the flow,
Every grain by thought is fanned,
Inspiration's gentle glow.

With every turn, a new dawn breaks,
Bringing forth the muse's song,
In endless cycles, creation wakes,
The artist's heart where echoes long.

Dreams find form in shifting hues,
Life breathes in poetic sighs,
Time and muse their path renews,
In the hourglass where moment flies.

In the dance of timeless grace,
The muse's hourglass revolves,
In every grain, the universe's face,
Bound by the mysteries it solves.

Threads of Fantasy

In a realm where shadows dance,
Underneath the twilight's trance.
Stars ignite with whispered themes,
Woven tight in silken dreams.

Mystic rivers ebb and flow,
Through the woods of indigo.
Tethers of a wishful night,
Guide the heart to boundless light.

Fantasy's embroidered threads,
Form a web above our heads.
Each a tale of might and grace,
Spun in time, an endless lace.

Glimpses of a world unseen,
In the fabric, bold and keen.
Truth and myth entwined as one,
Waltzing till the night is done.

Every dream and whispered sigh,
Threads of fantasy, they fly.
Crafting worlds beyond our reach,
Touched by magic's tender breach.

Hushed Epiphanies

In the quiet, truths unveil,
Soft as feather, pale and frail.
Gentle murmurs of the heart,
Secrets whisper, lives depart.

Moments edged in silent gold,
Wisdom ancient, stories old.
Learned in the calm of night,
Glimmers faint in moon's soft light.

Epiphanies in shades of gray,
Hover as the dawn of day.
Silent echoes in the breeze,
Whispers rustling through the trees.

Thoughts align like twilight's beam,
Subtle as a muted dream.
Every heart beat, every breath,
Speaks a truth beyond mere death.

In the hush where magic lies,
Hidden realms of sound disguise.
Epiphanies in shadow's glide,
Guide us to the light inside.

Cocooned in Whispers

In a shell of hushed delight,
Cocooned whispers in the night.
Softly guiding, subtly clear,
Drawing nigh the dreams held dear.

Murky shadows kiss our skins,
Muffled voices, distant sins.
Hold us in a gentle grip,
Cradle us on twilight's lip.

Warmth of secrecy encloses,
As the starlit night disposes.
Gentle hum of unseen wings,
Wraps us close with hidden strings.

Nested deep in velvety sound,
Whispered secrets all around.
Words that float on tender air,
Echo love's unspoken prayer.

As the night bestows its charm,
Cocooned whispers keep us warm.
Into dawn, from evening's start,
Guiding dreams, be still, dear heart.

Labyrinthine Muse

In the maze of thoughts uncharted,
Thrives a muse, pure-hearted.
Winds her way through lanes obscure,
Crafting tales both rich and pure.

Shadows curve and twist in line,
Paths unknown seem so benign.
Every turn a cryptic clue,
Secrets whispered, old and new.

Within walls of ivy green,
Labyrinthine spleen unseen.
Births a song from silken strings,
A muse that moves with unseen wings.

Every passage, every choice,
Echoes with her haunting voice.
Guides the lost through shaded halls,
Hears the call as nightfall crawls.

In this labyrinth of hues,
Dwells the spirit of the muse.
Inspiration bound and free,
Leads us to our destiny.

Choreography of Thoughts

In the theater of my mind,
Ideas dance and intertwine.
Pirouettes of past and new,
A ballet in thoughts' revue.

Each notion a careful step,
In rhythms that we adept.
Chasing shadows, seeking light,
Dreams evolve in silent night.

Stirrings of the deep unknown,
In this dance, my seeds are sown.
Patterns weave and thoughts align,
In the space where visions shine.

A medley of hopes and fears,
Flowing through the hidden spheres.
Mind's choreography revealed,
In the dance, my fate is sealed.

Ebb and flow of mental streams,
Orchestrate the mind's grand schemes.
Thoughts become a flowing tide,
In this dance, we all confide.

A Journey Through Dreams

Under stars, the night unfolds,
Dreamscapes where the heart beholds.
Wander far, past known realms,
In dreamland, my spirit helms.

Mountains tall, and valleys wide,
In this land, we do not hide.
Colors more than eyes can see,
In dreams, all my fears set free.

Through the clouds, I drift away,
Castles in the sky, we stay.
Unseen worlds beneath the sea,
Dreams that set our souls to spree.

Mystic beings whisper light,
Guiding us through endless night.
In this space, with time unbound,
Dreams weave universes round.

A journey through unconscious streams,
Life reflected in moonbeams.
In these dreams, the truth is clear,
Fantasies and hopes adhere.

Nebula of Nostalgia

Swirling mists of memories lost,
In nebulae where time's embossed.
Echoes of the days gone by,
Blend with starlight in the sky.

Fractured fragments, old and bright,
Dancing on the edge of night.
In this nebula of gold,
Stories of our lives unfold.

Shadows of the cherished times,
Linger in nostalgic rhymes.
Galaxies of joy and pain,
Twist in nebulous refrain.

Every sigh and laughter's hue,
Stars that formed the past we knew.
In this cosmic lullaby,
Nostalgia's whispers never die.

As we drift in times before,
Crafting myths forevermore.
Nebula of thoughts unsaid,
Light the path where memories tread.

Symphony of Silence

In the hush, a world unfolds,
Where silence its own story holds.
Every pause, a note so clear,
Symphonies for those who hear.

In the stillness of the night,
Quiet whispers bring delight.
Silent reveries abound,
In this peace, true solace found.

Moments where the world stands still,
Voices soft, a gentle thrill.
Harmony in silent air,
Breathes a song beyond compare.

Eloquence in every pause,
Silent truths without a cause.
In the void, an orchestra,
Playing life's own cadenza.

Symphony of silence calls,
In its grace, the heart enthralls.
Sounds unseen, in quiet grace,
Echo through the empty space.

Hidden Sanctuaries

In gardens where the shadows play,
There lies a path less known,
Where whispered secrets softly lay,
In corners overgrown.

Beneath the arch of autumn's gold,
Amongst the fallen leaves,
The tales of yore and dreams of old,
Mingle like evening eves.

A bench where silences converse,
With echoes of the past,
Wraps around the universe,
In memories that last.

By moonlit streams and quiet nooks,
Where time itself stands still,
Sheltered from the scribe of books,
A heart can drink its fill.

These hidden sanctuaries found,
In moments soft and rare,
Where peace and stillness most abound,
Become our secret lair.

Cradled by Starlit Skies

Under a cosmic, gleaming quilt,
In silence deep as seas,
The dreams and hopes of hearts are built,
On night's celestial breeze.

Lulled by twinkling, distant fires,
And tales that stars compose,
We're cradled by our own desires,
As night around us flows.

Each star a whisper, soft and sweet,
In that grand, eternal night,
Echoes of a cosmic beat,
In silent, tranquil light.

Above, the heavens sing their praise,
In constellations bright,
While wrapped in night's embracing haze,
We journey in our flight.

Cradled in this ethereal space,
Our spirits drift and soar,
Through vast expanses, hints of grace,
Infinity's grand door.

Of Dreams and Soft Murmurs

In realms where shadows softly breathe,
And whispers fill the night,
We wander paths we scarcely leave,
In dreams that take to flight.

Soft murmurs of a distant past,
Echo beneath the moon,
Where fleeting moments fade too fast,
Yet sing a haunting tune.

In slumbers deep, we dance with time,
To melodies unseen,
With hearts that grasp a silent rhyme,
In realms of in-between.

Each dream a tale, a voyage grand,
Through seas of endless stars,
We reach for lands of timeless sand,
And hearts without the scars.

Let dreams and whispers guide us true,
Through night's serene embrace,
To find a dawn both bright and new,
In morning's gentle grace.

Beneath the Wishing Tree

There stands a tree in quiet glade,
With branches old and wide,
Where wishes made and promises laid,
By time are gently tied.

Beneath its shade, the dreams do grow,
Of hearts both young and old,
In whispered prayers and hopes that glow,
Their stories silently told.

The leaves, they shimmer in the breeze,
With secrets, hopes, and dreams,
A lullaby within the trees,
In sunlight's golden beams.

Each branch a world of silent grace,
Each root a wish held fast,
Time cannot erase this place,
Nor shadows it has cast.

So come and sit, beneath the boughs,
In quiet, blissful peace,
Let your heart make silent vows,
And feel all burdens cease.